better together*

This book is best read together, grownup and kid.

 akidsco.com

a
kids
book
about

a kids book about

PRONOUNS

by Dr. Courtney Wells & Lee Wells

a
kids
book
about

Printed in the United States of America.

A Kids Book About books are available online: *akidsco.com*

To share your stories, ask questions, or inquire about bulk
purchases (schools, libraries, and nonprofits), please use
the following email address: *hello@akidsco.com*

Print ISBN: 978-1-958825-39-6
Ebook ISBN: 978-1-958825-40-2

Designed by Rick DeLucco
Edited by Emma Wolf

Hi, kids!
Remember you are valuable,
lovable, and amazing just as you are.

Intro

Why do pronouns matter? For some, this question may be uncomfortable and confusing. It's OK if you don't know how to answer it! Pronouns are a tricky topic, influenced by our culture, backgrounds, societal beliefs, and systemic oppression.

Pronouns are some of the smallest words in length, yet they can have a profound impact on kids' mental health and self-worth. When grownups learn about and use kids' pronouns correctly, they have a direct impact on their wellness. Just like using someone's name can show respect, correctly using someone's pronouns honors their dignity and demonstrates their value.

This book won't (and can't) give you all the answers as language is always evolving and changing—and everyone's experience with pronouns is unique. What we do know is that you opened this book. This small action shows your willingness to learn, change, and build more inclusive environments for all kids.

I'm Courtney.

And I use they/them pronouns.

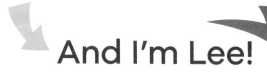

And I'm Lee!

I use she/her pronouns.

You might have noticed
that we introduced ourselves
with something called...

PRONOUNS.

Why did we do that?

Because identifying
our pronouns is a part of
identifying who we are!

You wouldn't know our pronouns from our names, and even if you could see what we look like, you still wouldn't know what our pronouns are!

So, what are pronouns?

A pronoun is a word we use
to stand in for a noun (in this
case, we're talking about people).

A pronoun says, "Hey, I see you! Even when I'm not using your name."

 Here are some examples:

THEY/THEM

HE/HIM

SHE/HER

HE/SHE/THEY

THEY/SHE

ZE/ZIR★

XE/XEM

FAE/FAER

NE/NEM/NEARS

ELLE (in SPANISH)

Some people use their name only,
and no pronouns! And this is
definitely not all of them!

Why are there so many different pronouns?

Because everyone is unique.
And everyone feels a specific way
about themselves and how they
express who they are.

Language is really
important to humans.

And the more words we have, the more options we have to explain who we are to ourselves and others.

Sometimes, the world will tell us there are only 2 options: she and he (that's called the binary).

But that's not really true
to how people feel and
experience the world!

At the beginning of our lives, pronouns are assumed for us based on the sex we're assigned at birth by a doctor.

But as we explore, grow, and learn more about ourselves, sometimes those pronouns don't match how we feel.

And that's OK!

Just because someone tells us doesn't mean that's what

our gender when we're born,
we know ourselves to be.

Pronouns are about being...

you

and being seen and existing in
all parts of language as you are.

For example, imagine if your name was Lee, and everywhere you went, everybody called you Courtney.

That would feel SO frustrating, wouldn't it?

Or maybe isolating, confusing, or upsetting.

Well, the same thing happens when someone consistently uses the wrong pronouns for you.

It hurts as much as people calling you the wrong name.

When people teach that there are only 2 options for pronouns—and that isn't true—we can feel confused and uncertain.

One of the best things
we can do when we're not
sure about something is
ask questions about it.

_____

Learning new things brings discomfort, but that isn't a bad thing. It's an opportunity to grow!

All kinds of growing can feel uncomfortable. But growing pains are a sign of evolving, and that's a great thing.

As you're learning and changing, making mistakes is inevitable.

But we can honor and recognize someone for who they are by sticking with it and trying again.

We know you believe every person is valuable, important, and deserving of love.

One way we show how much we care for others is by asking about and then using their correct pronouns.

And you can start today!

Kids, we have some
really cool news for you.

You are going to be an expert in knowing this stuff, while grownups are mostly beginners!

Our brains store new information as we learn (even if it's unhelpful).

And we can't really unlearn
that unhelpful information.

So, grownups...well, you have
a bit more work to do. Get ready
to feel uncomfortable!

You will need to ask for help in understanding different pronouns and why they're important to people, even when it's hard.

You're going to make mistakes, even when you practice. You'll get it wrong, and try again.

(Believe us—we still make mistakes.)

Remember our friend Lee?

Imagine if you'd never
met them before.

Would you assume
their name was Lee?

How would you even know?

Pronouns are exactly the same!

Often our assumptions are rooted in that older, unhelpful learning.

In order to begin new learning, we need to practice asking!

It's not about being right all the time; it's about being loving with the effort. And trust us, people notice when you make the effort.

Kids, maybe some of you have new pronouns.

Or maybe you're thinking about using different pronouns.

Or maybe you don't even know which pronouns fit.

We hope you know how **OK** that is!

It's OK if today is the first time you're thinking about pronouns.

It's **OK** if reading this book has made you feel scared, excited, confused, or something else entirely.

It's **OK** if you feel like your pronouns change every day (or every hour!).

It's **OK** to feel worried that other people may not understand.

It's **OK** to be exactly
who you are today.

And if that changes tomorrow,
that's **OK** too.

And if it changes again,
that's OK too.

And if it never changes,
that's **OK** too.

And no matter which pronouns you use (if you use any!), you are important, loveable, valuable, and no matter how much you change,

THAT NEVER WILL.

Outro

Talking about pronouns can feel like we stepped into quicksand. The more we struggle to get out, the quicker we sink. Do you know how to get out of quicksand? Lean back, stretch out, and make as much contact with it as possible—and you will rise to the surface. Just like leaning into quicksand, the more contact you have with pronouns, the more comfortable you will be asking about and using them.

As therapists, we know that kids learn a lot by watching and listening to the grownups around them. When grownups make mistakes and rebound, kids learn that it's OK to make mistakes too. When grownups use inclusive language, kids learn that they have supportive, accepting people to turn to. When you read books like this together, kids learn that they can have important conversations with you.

So go ahead and read this book again!

About The Authors

Dr. Courtney Wells (they/them) and Lee Wells, LCSW (she/her), wrote this book for their family. At the time, they were growing their family through adoption. For Courtney, being a trans, nonbinary parent amidst near-constant anti-LGBTQ+ legislation and media, it felt important that their family and community have access to information and ways to talk about pronouns. Lee, of course, couldn't agree more!

As therapists, Lee and Courtney know there are many sources of knowing, growing, and healing—books are one such source! Kids' books are collaborative pathways to start (and continue) conversations between grownups and kids, often with some joy and humor. Take it from 2 therapists: compassionate, fact-forward conversations build stronger parent-child relationships AND more just and inclusive communities.

 @mindchicago, @pivotpsychchicago

 www.mindchicago.com, www.pivotpsychchicago.org

kids book about
...ONEY
...tromosser

kids book about
BEING
INCLUSIVE
by Ashton Mota
& Rebekah Bruesehoff

kids book about
diversity

kids book about
LEADEr·
SHIP
by Orion Jean

kids bo... ab...
IMM...
by MJ Ca...

a kids book about
SAFETY
y Soraya Sutherlin, CEM
partnership with JUBY

a kids book about
CLIMATE
CHANGE
by Zanagee Artis
Olivia Greenspan

a kids book about
IMAGINATION
by **LEVAR BURTON**

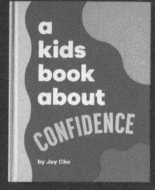
a kids book about
CONFIDENCE
by Joy Cho

ls ok out
KIETY
abo
Happy Faces

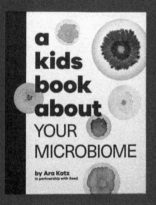
a kids book about
YOUR
MICROBIOME
by Ara Katz
in partnership with Seed

a kids book about
racism
by Jelani Memory

a kids book about
DISABILITIES
by Kristine Napper

a ki
b ab bo
by: KYLE

a kids book about
VORCE
Ashley Simpo

a kids book about
cancer
by Dr. Kelsie Storm & Sarah Porter

a kids book about
BEING
TRANSGENDER
by Gia Parr
in partnership with *The GenderCool Project*

a kids book about
DEPRESSION
by Kileah McIlvain

ls ok out
ame

a kids book about
THE TULSA

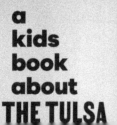

Discover more at akidsco.com